To my daughter Alice, with all ı

Magic Sparkles have been used the cakes in this book. They are edible and safe to use on ⸱kes.
They can be used on cakes, sweets, chocolates or desserts for a special touch.
Use straight from the pot or grind down to a finer glitter. To do this, either leave in the pot ⸱
mortar. To attach to cakes the surface should be tacky not wet – if too wet they will dissolv ⸱⸱ow, is ideal although you
can use water or alcohol. Their appearance is enhanced by good lighting - halogen or spotlights work well.

How To Use The Size Guide (CC)

On any instructions for modelling in this book I have used the Cel Cakes Size Guide. This should make it easier to produce proportioned figures. To achieve the correct size, the ball of paste should sit in the correct hole (size below it) with 1/3 of the paste showing out of the bottom and 2/3 out of the top (this does not apply to the smallest sizes). You will then have approximately the correct size ball of paste to shape.

NOTE: **ANY SPECIAL EQUIPMENT USED HAS A SUPPLIER CODE. FOR EXAMPLE – SIZE GUIDE (CC) – SUPPLIER CEL CAKES. SEE ACKNOWLEDGMENTS PAGE 37 .**

Recipes

Modelling Paste

Either:- 1/2 sugarpaste 1/2 flower paste kneaded together, or knead 5ml (1tsp) of gum tragacanth into 225g (8ozs) sugarpaste and leave for 8 hours, or knead 5ml (1tsp) Tylo (CMC) powder into 225g (8ozs) sugarpaste.

Mexican Paste

Mix together 225g (8ozs) of icing sugar and 3 level teaspoons of gum tragacanth. Add 25ml (5tsp) of cold water (taken from tap). Mix together, turnout and knead well. Store in a plastic bag and a sealed container for 6-8 hours to mature. The paste will feel very hard but will soften up easily. Break off small pieces and soften in your fingers. Matured paste will freeze.

Royal Icing

Place 30ml (6 level tsp) of merriwhite in a mixing bowl and gradually add 5tbs cold water mixing with a wooden spoon until free from lumps. Add 225g (8ozs) of icing sugar and mix until smooth. Add 110g (4ozs) of icing sugar and then add the rest gradually until the correct consistency is reached. Beat well for approximately 5 minutes. Store in the fridge, in an airtight container. It should keep for 4 weeks.

Softened Sugarpaste

Place the amount of sugarpaste you want to soften in a bowl. Chop up roughly and then gradually add drops of cold water. Break down with a fork or a spoon and mix until smooth and lump free. Continue until required consistency is reached. The first time you do this, be careful not to add too much water too soon. It softens quickly.

Sugar Glue

This is easily made with 1 part Tylo (CMC) powder to 25-30 parts water. Place the powder in a bottle or jar that has a lid. Add the water, replace the lid and shake. There will be thick creamy white pieces in the water. They will dissolve and the liquid will become clear by the following day.

25cm x 20cm (10 x 8in) Rich fruit cake covered with Shell Pink Regalice, 36cm x 30cm (14 x 12in) cake board, Mexican paste, white sugarpaste, edible glue (P1), a little royal icing, white Magic Sparkles ground finer (P1) (JK), Trex, edible glue (p1), isopropyl alcohol.

Paste Colours: Bulrush, Violet, Rose, Gentian, Mint (SK).

Dust colours: Dusky Pink (SF), Snowflake Lustre, Gentian, Violet, Marigold, Silver (SK).

Birds, large and small teddies from Make a Cradle set (PC), booties cutter from Nursery set (PC), Butterfly cutter (PC), ABC block embosser (HP), small raw silk rolling pin (HP), mini embroidery embosser (HP), small and medium blossom cutters from set of three (FMM), bow cutter (FMM), rabbit cutter – Tappits set (FMM), stitch wheel (PME), frilling stick (Jem), dresden tool, small heart cutter, circle cutter 3cm, non stick rolling pin and board, fine paintbrush, No.1 & no.2 piping nozzles, small sharp knife, greaseproof paper,.

1 Cut out approximately 60 medium and 12 small blossoms in Mexican paste and leave to dry.

2 For washing line, draw a curve on greaseproof paper. Lay the paper over cake to check for position of each line. Cut along line then lay over cake again and mark with a sharp knife. Colour a little royal icing grey and using a no.1 nozzle, pipe the two lines. When dry mix silver powder with isopropyl alcohol and paint.

3 Trace the clothes patterns on p36 and cut out. Colour Mexican paste in required colours and cut out clothes. It is best to grease the non stick rolling board with trex then roll out paste – do not lift and turn. Grease back of pattern with a little trex, lay on paste then cut out. Mark clothes as shown, with stitch wheel, embossers, dresden tool etc. Place on a sponge pad and leave to dry. The cardigan should be cut out in sugarpaste and marked with a dresden tool. Mark vertical lines first.

4 For the birds, teddy and booties roll out Mexican paste as before. Grease the cutters with trex then cut out and leave to dry.

5 Roll out Mexican paste for the bibs. Cut out with a circle cutter. Emboss then either frill with a frilling stick, mark with a stitch wheel or leave plain to pipe an edge when attached to cake.

6 To paint clothes or toys, mix powder colours with isopropyl alcohol and use a fine paintbrush. Birds are dusted with dry powder colour. All clothes and toys are then dusted with snowflake. To add magic sparkles, brush thinly with glue and then sprinkle on over greaseproof paper so excess can be returned to pot.

7 Colour Mexican paste light brown. Roll out to 2mm thick. Cut long straight lines 2mm apart. Next, cut across at 8mm to make pegs. Emboss a line 5mm down each peg. Place pegs on a pad to dry.

8 Position clothes and toys under each line. Using a no.1 nozzle, attach clothes with royal icing. Pipe bib ties and bib edge. Attach birds and pegs.

9 Colour some royal icing pale green and place in a piping bag. Cut a small v at tip. Pipe a small leaf at base of cake then attach a medium blossom. Repeat around cake. Pipe three leaves on each corner of board and add three small blossoms. Colour a little royal icing pink, lilac and blue and pipe into the centres of blossoms. When dry, Brush all flowers and leaves lightly with edible glue and cover with magic sparkles.

10 Colour royal icing grey and using a no.1 nozzle starting at the centre back of board, pipe the words 'sugar and spice and all things nice, that's what little girls are made of'. Continue around board. Leave to dry and then paint silver.

Natalie

Teddy bear cake and small teddy bear cake (see below), 36cm (14in) oval board, 900g (2lb) Celebration Regalice, 900g sugarpaste, 300g (11oz) flower paste, royal icing, edible glue (p1), isopropyl alcohol, sieved apricot jam.

Paste Colours: Lilac, Bulrush, black (SK).

Powder Colours: Snowflake Lustre, Bulrush, Blue (SK), Dusky Pink (SF).

Cake Tins: Stand-Up Cuddly Bear Set and Mini Stand Up Bear Pan Set (Wilton – PME), Diamond Side Embosser (PC), small teddy from Make a Cradle set (PC), small raw silk rolling pin (HP), Wilton nozzle no.233 plus piping bag and adaptor (PME), 2cm (1/2 in) double curve serrated crimper (PME), plain or serrated bow crimper (PME), paint and dusting brushes, bow cutter (FMM), small heart cutter (FMM), Dresden tool.

1 Check the quantity of sponge cake mixture you usually use with the tin size. Do this by filling each half of the teddy tins with water and then pouring into your cake tins to see what size mix you will need. Follow the instructions given with the tins on how to use and bake.

2 Cover board with Celebration Regalice. Emboss with the diamond embosser then the Dresden tool onto corners of each diamond. Emboss the teddy into alternate rows of diamonds. Use the bow crimper around edge of board. Dust teddies with brown powder colour and then over whole board with snowflake lustre.

3 Trim arms off large teddy. Colour 100g of sugarpaste pale brown with paste colour. Brush apricot jam on inside of both teddies ears, snout and soles of feet, then roll out pieces of paste to cover.

4 Place large teddy towards back half of board. Mix together 250g each of flower

paste and sugarpaste and colour with lilac paste colour. Roll out and cut a 36cm diameter circle. Take out a centre circle of approximately 13cm diameter. Cut an opening from centre circle to outside edge. Place dress around teddy to check for size, trim as necessary. Crimp edge and emboss with bow cutter. Brush cake with apricot jam and position dress.

5 Mix together 50g each of sugarpaste and flower paste. Roll out a third and on the final roll, use the silk rolling pin. Cut out two pieces for a collar and crimp edge. Attach to dress with edible glue. Roll remaining paste into long strips. Use silk rolling pin before cutting to 3cm wide. Cut two tails each 8cm long. Cut one end of each diagonally. Gather straight ends and attach to back of dress with glue. Cut two pieces 16cm long and gather at each end, fold in half and attach to dress. Cut out a piece 6cm long, gather each end, tuck one end over joins of bow loops and other end under bow loops. Place some kitchen paper into loops until dry. When dry, dust bow, dress and collar with snowflake.

6 Colour some sugarpaste black. Shape a nose and two eyes, then attach with glue. Mix snowflake and isopropyl alcohol and paint a highlight to each. Paint a black line from nose and two curves at end for mouth. Using pink powder colour and a dusting brush, colour inside ears, cheeks and feet.

7 Colour enough sugarpaste brown for arms (this brown should now match the colour the teddy's fur will be piped). Attach the left arm with glue to the dress. Roll out lilac trimmings from dress and cut out enough paste for a sleeve and attach to top of arm.

8 Colour some royal icing brown. Using the piping bag, adaptor and nozzle start to pipe the fur. Practise first on some spare sugarpaste. Start to squeeze the icing out a little and touch to cake. Squeeze a little

more then stop squeezing before pulling nozzle away. Do not have the icing too soft or overfill the piping bag. Start at the back of teddy's head and always pipe the fur at the lowest point side to side and work your way up.

9 The instructions for the baby teddy are the same but add a sugarpaste nappy to front and back and use lighter colour icing when piping fur. Decorate the little teddy on a separate board. Before piping the fur, cover the nappy with softened sugarpaste (see p1). Use a damp paintbrush to spread and then make fluffy. Shape the bottle from sugarpaste. Add a small heart to the front, shape a teat to add to the top, then a band over join of teat and bottle. Paint colours on by mixing powder colours with isopropyl alcohol. Position bottle on baby with royal icing. Leave to dry and then place in front of large teddy. Add large teddy's right arm so it rests on the baby. Add the sleeve and pipe fur as before.

Mark

20cm (8in) Square marzipanned rich fruit cake, 28cm (11in) board, 1.3kg (3lb) Baby Blue Regalice, 450g (1lb) white sugarpaste, 150g (5oz) marzipan, edible glue (see p1), isopropyl alcohol.

Paste Colours: Paprika, Pink (SF), Bulrush, Gentian, Marigold (SK).

Powder Colours: Snowflake Lustre, Black, White (SK), Dusky Pink (SF).

Double curve serrated crimper 2cm ($^1/_2$ in) (PME), small heart cutter, 3cm circle cutter, no.2 and no.4 piping nozzles, dresden tool, veining tool for a five or six petal flower (Jem), size 0 & 4 paintbrushes, flat dusting brush, satay stick, size guide (see p1),(CC).

1 Place cake on board. Ice cake thinner than usual with blue Regalice. Crimp around three of the top edges. Ice board with white sugarpaste.

2 For left and right cake sides, divide and mark each side horizontally into six equal sections. Roll one white and two blue sausages of sugarpaste for each side each weighing approximately 42g. Slice in half lengthways and check that each piece will fit onto one of the sixth markings on side of cake. Start with two blue halves along bottom of cake, two white in centre, then two blue to finish at top. Attach with edible glue.

3 Mark front and back of cake sides into three. Roll out two blue and one white sausage of sugarpaste each 130g. They should be long enough to cover ends of paste on left and right sides. Slice in half lengthways and attach to front and back of cake covering ends on left and right. Leave to dry.

4 Soften baby blue Regalice (see p1) and place in a piping bag. Pipe over cake, spreading out with a damp paintbrush. Work on areas approximately 10cm x 10cm at a time. Fluff out icing with the paintbrush to resemble a towel. Work all over cake hiding top edge of cake that isn't crimped and disguising edge of rolls around cake sides.Repeat with softened white sugarpaste, covering middle layer and cake board.

5 Using the size guide, roll a size 16 ball of white sugarpaste. Place ball of paste on worktop and shape the nappy from this upside down. Push in at the front and back. Pinch the top at sides where legs will be attached. Keep pressing down to the worktop to make flat across top of nappy in order for baby's body to be attached neatly. Turn nappy right way up and add a triangle of sugarpaste to the front attaching with glue.

6 Colour marzipan flesh colour using paprika and a little pink.Legs are each a size 12 of marzipan. Roll a sausage, flatten slightly at thigh, place in palm of hand, roll small finger across at knee and ankle to shape. Bend up foot and pinch slightly to flatten and shape. Mark two lines round ankle and two or three creases at sides of knees with a dresden tool. Add dimples to knees with a paintbrush handle. Attach legs with a little glue to nappy. Push a satay stick measuring 8cm into top of nappy. Roll tiny balls of marzipan for toes. Make 10 and then put them in pairs in order of size before attaching with glue.

7 Using a size 15 ball of marzipan, shape for body. Press down onto worktop, flattening at front and back. Attach to nappy with glue, pushing over satay stick. Mark belly button with a veining tool, chest with a dresden tool and paintbrush handle.

8 Use a size 9 ball of flower paste for the talcum powder. Press into shape then emboss with a small heart cutter. Brush heart with pink powder colour. Roll a small ball of flower paste and press between finger and thumb. Mark around sides with a sharp knife. Attach to top of talcum powder with glue. Mark holes on top with a cocktail stick.

9 Head is a size 16 ball of marzipan. Attach to body over skewer. Emboss mouth with a circle cutter, pulling down bottom lip slightly. Emboss corners of mouth with a no.4 piping nozzle.

10 Make holes for eyes with a paintbrush handle and fill in with small balls of white flowerpaste. Colour a little flower paste blue with gentian and attach a small ball of flattened paste to each eye. Paint in pupils with black powder mixed with isopropyl alcohol then paint a tiny white dot into each eye.

11 Add a tiny ball of marzipan for nose. Dust cheeks with a little pink powder. Paint eyebrows and eyelashes with bulrush. Make six to eight holes in top of head with a cocktail stick. Colour a little marzipan brown and from very small balls of this, roll fine strands for hair and place in holes.

12 Arms are each shaped from size 12 balls of marzipan. Roll thinner at top then shape elbow and wrist. Pinch hand flatter, cut a v out to separate thumb from fingers. Mark fingers with a knife and nails with a no.2 nozzle. Mark creases at wrist and elbows as before. Add dimples to hands. Brush glue thinly at top of arms, side of head, in hands and at back of talc. Attach talc to top of head then arms to body, up sides of head and hands on to talc.

13 Pipe some softened sugarpaste to centre of cake and attach baby. Colour a little flower paste yellow and a little grey. Roll grey long and thin, make a loop in the centre and bring ends up to the same end. Shape a curve in yellow. Attach both parts of pin to the nappy with glue. Pipe softened sugarpaste over nappy and using a damp paintbrush, spread and make fluffy. Place some icing sugar in a small sieve. Place above baby's head then gently tap against talc pot until enough 'talc' has spilt.

Laura

18cm (7in) Square rich fruit cake, 30.5cm (12in) cake board, 600g (1½lb) marzipan, 900g (2lb) sugarpaste, 450g (1lb) modelling paste (see p1), Mexican paste, royal icing, edible glue (p1), isopropyl alcohol, Trex.

Paste Colours: Bulrush, Gentian, Rose, Violet, Mint, Marigold, Black (SK), Paprika (SF).

Powder Colours: Snowflake lustre, White, Gentian (SK), Dusky Pink (SF).

Small raw silk rolling pink (HP), Large watermark taffeta rolling pin (HP), 2cm (½ in) and 1.2cm (½ in) double curve serrated crimper (PME), easy twist alphabets upper and lower (PC), make a cradle set (PC), Quilting embosser (PC), Straight frill / lace cutter LA1 (OP), Frilling stick / mouth tool (JEM), teddy bear's picnic mould (DP), no.2 piping nozzle, size guide (see p1) (CC), Dresden tool, sparkling ribbon, oblong cocktail stick box, non stick rolling pin and board.

1 Colour 700g of sugarpaste light brown and cover the board. Roll the taffeta rolling pin over then trim excess sugarpaste. Use either a size guide or a ruler and mark floorboards 2.5cm apart. Using a dresden tool, mark the planks of wood across randomly.

2 Cut the cake in half. Place one half on top of the other and cover with marzipan. Cover with sugarpaste and place on board.

3 To make the canopy support, roll out a strip of Mexican paste to 3mm thick. Cut out a strip measuring 20cm x 5cm. Bend into an arch shape and support over a curve or sponge and kitchen paper but keep ends approximately 9-10cm apart – check the size with the width of your cake. The height of the arch should be approximately 8cm.

4 Roll out Mexican paste and cut a strip 4cm wide and long enough to fit around top edge of cake. Using royal icing, attach around top edge of cake and support until dry.

5 Using the size guide, shape a pillow from a size 15 ball of sugarpaste. Use the small crimper around edge and hollow a little where baby's head will rest. Check it will fit under the drying arch before attaching to top end of cradle with edible glue.

6 Use a size 15 ball of sugapaste for baby's body, shape and place on cradle. Colour some modelling paste pale pink. Roll out and before embossing with the quilter, roll with the raw silk rolling pin. Cut around edge then lay over baby's body stretching a little if needed. Brush top of quilt with glue, then roll out a strip of modelling paste measuring 10cm x 3cm. Frill one edge with the frilling stick. Attach to top end of quilt, folding the straight edge over quilt.

7 Colour a size 12 ball of marzipan for head and enough for a hand, nose and ears, flesh colour with a little paprika and pink. Secure head to pillow with glue. Emboss mouth with tool. Dust cheeks with pink powder. Roll a small ball of paste for nose and attach. Press the frilling stick into head to make holes for eyes and fill with small balls of modelling paste. Colour a small piece of modelling paste black and attach a tiny piece to each eye. Paint a small white dot by mixing powder colour with isopropyl alcohol. Paint eyelashes and eyebrows. Shape two ears and attach. Make several small holes on top of head with a cocktail stick. Colour a little marzipan brown. Roll tiny balls of marzipan into small thin strands of hair and push into holes. Shape a hand from a size 5. The sleeve is a size 8. Attach sleeve and hand.

8 Attach arch above baby's head with royal icing. Leave to dry.

9 Roll out long strips of modelling paste. Do the final roll with the raw silk rolling pin. Cut one edge straight then cut the strip 6cm wide with the lace cutter. Cut a hole in each point with a no.2 nozzle. Brush glue 5-6cm from base of cake all around. Pick up frill and pleat together a little along straight edge as you attach the frill from the back. At the end of each piece, fold edge under and start the next piece with the edge folded under to disguise the join. Attach the second frill layer between top of the bottom frill and top edge of cradle sides. Finish with the third frill and add a lace edge at the top in very pale pink modelling paste. This is achieved by rolling a long thin strip and a final roll with the silk rolling pin, then cutting both edges as close as possible with the lace cutter. Cut the holes and then attach over edge with glue. Crimp around top with the small crimper.

10 For the canopy, roll out modelling paste and use the raw silk rolling pin for the final roll, then cut out an oblong measuring 30cm x 13cm – cut one long edge straight and three with the lace cutter. Cut holes as before and then gather along straight edge. Brush top and sides of arch thinly with glue. Fold gathered edge in half and then place over arch. Add a lace trim to the top of canopy to match top edge of cradle sides. Leave to dry.

11 Knead a small piece of marzipan and press into teddy mould. Release and leave to dry. Dust bow, paint eyes, nose and mouth, then dust body with brown powder. Dust over whole bear with snowflake and place in cradle next to baby. Dust cake with snowflake lustre and attach a ribbon bow with royal icing to top of canopy.

CONTINUED...

12 Colour a little Mexican paste pink. Grease a non stick board and the three cutters for the dolls cradle from the make a cradle set with trex. Roll out the Mexican paste thinly and cut out the three cradle pieces. Emboss with the stork and small teddy. Dry cradle base over a cocktail stick box, or a shaped former. Cut out the bow trim in white Mexican paste and attach to headboard. Leave all pieces to dry.

13 Attach three cradle pieces together with royal icing. Place on cake board and support underneath. Leave to dry. Using sugarpaste shape a tiny pillow and place in cradle. Colour a little paste lilac for body and place in cradle. For the blanket, roll out a small piece of modelling paste 5cm x 3cm and emboss with rolling pin, stork and crimp edge. Colour enough marzipan flesh for arms and head. Shape arms, attach and add a little sleeve to each. Shape and attach head. Mark mouth with the tool, add a tiny nose and mark eyes with a cocktail stick dipped in paste colour. Shape hair from pieces of marzipan marked with a knife. Dust cheeks and add bows to hair. Dust dress and blanket with snowflake.

14 The sheep's body is a size 11 ball of white modelling paste. Add four size 7 balls of paste for legs and a size 8 for head. Add a tiny tail. Mark eyes with a cocktail stick as before. Leave to dry. Paint feet black. Place a no.2 nozzle in a piping bag and pipe curl shapes all over sheep omitting face. Ears are shaped, hollowed with a paintbrush handle, dusted pink and then attached. Add a tiny grey nose. Leave to dry then dust with snowflake lustre avoiding face.

15 The large duck is modelled from the following sizes of sugarpaste or modelling paste: body 11, head 8, wings each size 6, beak 5, wheels each size 6. Reduce the size proportionately for the medium and small ducks. Mark holes in beaks with a cocktail stick. Mark eyes as before. Colour a little

royal icing brown and pipe a string with a no.1 nozzle joining ducks together.

16 Each of the building blocks is a 2.5cm cube of sugarpaste. Colour each in a pastel shade and shape into a cube. Crimp each edge and emboss with the letters for the child's name. Attach to board and each other with royal icing.

Michael

20cm (8in) Marzipanned rich fruit cake, 30.5cm (12in) cake board, 1kg (2$\frac{1}{2}$ lb) sugarpaste, flower paste, a little royal icing, 2 x Hint of Blue Magic Sparkles ground finer (see p1) (JK), edible glue (p1), isopropyl alcohol.

Paste Colours: Gentian, Marigold, Black (SK).

Powder Colours: Snowflake lustre (SK), Dusky Pink (SF).

Tappits toy set (FMM), no.1 & 2 piping nozzles, fine paintbrush, dusting brush, pastry brush, 3 white cotton stamens, size guide (see p1),(CC), mouth tool (Jem), small teddy from Make a Cradle set (PC), small heart cutter.

1 Place cake on board. Colour 700g of sugarpaste with gentian to match the magic sparkles colour and ice cake. Ice board with white sugarpaste.

2 Colour flower paste with gentian and cut out five each of the boat, aeroplane, rabbit, train and rocking horse. Leave to dry.

3 Using the pastry brush, cover cake with thin glue. Place cake over greaseproof paper and cover with sparkles. Remove excess from cake and board and place back in pot.

4 Position toys evenly around cake board. Secure with glue. When dry brush toys and board with snowflake lustre.

5 Colour 60g of sugarpaste pale yellow for the rabbit's body. Shape into a teardrop and flatten slightly. Attach to cake with glue. Emboss teddy and heart all over body.

6 Using the size guide shape feet each from a no.13 ball of sugarpaste. Arms are each size 11. Head is size 15, ears each size 11. Attach all with glue. Emboss a mouth with the embossing tool, joining two curves together at nose position. Roll a small ball of paste for nose and attach. Mark holes for eyes with a paintbrush handle.

7 Dust cheeks, nose, inside ears and feet with pink powder colour. Dust whole rabbit with snowflake lustre. Colour a little flower paste black and roll small balls of paste for eyes. Push into holes securing with a little glue. Mix snowflake powder with isopropyl alcohol and paint a small white dot to the left of each eye.

8 Cut tips off three stamens and cut in half to measure 1.25cm. Push into rabbit as whiskers. Place royal icing in a bag with a no.2 nozzle and pipe name. Pipe a small plain shell around base of cake.

Michael

Alex

20cm (8in) Marzipanned rich fruit cake, 28cm (11in) cake board, 1.1kg (2lb 8oz) sugarpaste, royal icing, flower paste, 2 x White & 1 x Hint of Lemon Magic Sparkles (JK), edible glue (p1), isopropyl alcohol.

Paste Colours: Egg Yellow (SF), Black (SK).

Powder Colours: Snowflake lustre, Marigold, Nasturtium (SK).

1.2cm ($1/2$in) double curve serrated crimper (PME), Straight frill cutter no.1 set 1(FMM), duck embosser from nursery set (HP), mini flower embossing set (HP), size guide (see p1) (CC), no.1 piping nozzle, frilling stick (Jem), stitch wheel (PME), Dresden tool, fine paintbrush.

1 Place marzipanned cake on board, cover with 700g of sugarpaste. Colour 175g with egg yellow and ice board. Crimp around edge of board.

2 Place white royal icing in a piping bag with a no.1 nozzle. Pipe a small plain shell around base of cake. Over pipe crimping.

3 For the band of paste around side, knead together equal quantities of flower paste and sugarpaste. Colour yellow and roll out a strip 5cm wide and long enough to fit around cake. Cut both edges with the straight frill cutter. Roll each edge with the frilling stick. Run the stitch wheel along edge of frilling. Emboss the duck and mini flower along centre of strip.

4 Brush glue around centre of side of cake. Roll up side strip and unroll around cake sides. Mix yellow and orange powder colours with isopropyl alcohol and paint ducks and flowers. When dry brush with snowflake lustre.

5 Colour 100g of sugarpaste yellow. The baby ducks feet are each shaped from a size 12 ball of yellow sugarpaste. Roll a ball, flatten slightly and mark front of feet with a knife. Attach to the cake with a little glue. Flatten more at back and brush with a little glue ready to attach body.

6 The body is a pear shape from 60g of sugarpaste. Attach over back of feet.

7 The wings are long teardrop shapes. Use a size 12 for each in white and a size 8 in yellow. Thin yellow piece around edge and then attach as the underside of wing. Attach to body.

8 The head is a size 15 ball of sugarpaste. Make a round ball, but point slightly at top of head and widen a little at cheeks. Attach to body.

9 Shape a beak from a size 11. Attach to head and mark with a dresden tool. Use a paintbrush handle to make holes for eyes. Colour a piece of flower paste black. Roll two small balls of paste for eyes and push into holes. Mix a little snowflake powder with isopropyl alcohol and paint a highlight in each eye.

10 Repeat instructions for large duck but in the following sizes: feet each size 14, body 130g, wings each size 30g, yellow under wing each size 12 – place one wing on small duck's back, head 60g, beak size 12.

11 Grind the hint of lemon magic sparkles finer (see p1). Place cake over greaseproof paper. Brush yellow parts of ducks very thinly with glue. Sprinkle with yellow sparkles. Any that fall onto the cake can be brushed off with a dry brush and replaced in the pot.

12 Leave white sparkles as large flakes and attach. For awkward angles, place on a dry brush and attach.

Joe

20cm (8in) Rich fruit cake iced with baby blue Regalice, 28cm (11in) cake drum, 225g (1/2 lb) modelling paste, size 14 (using the size guide) ball of marzipan coloured flesh with paprika (SF) and rose (SK) paste colours, small piece of marzipan for hair coloured with bulrush, white Magic Sparkles (JK), isopropyl alcohol, edible glue (p1).

Paste Colours: Black, Bulrush, Gentian, Marigold (SK).

Powder Colours: Snowflake Lustre, Silver (SK) Dusky Pink (SF).

No.2 & 3 piping nozzles, paintbrush size 3, small bow cutter (FMM), size guide (see p1), (CC).

1 Place iced cake on board. Ice board with baby blue Regalice.

2 Soften a small piece of baby blue Regalice with water (see p1). Place in a piping bag with a no.2 nozzle and pipe a small plain shell around base of cake.

3 Brush edible glue over iced board. Place cake over greaseproof paper and cover board with sparkles. Place excess sparkles back in pot or a pestle and mortar and grind finer (p1).

4 Mix snowflake powder with isopropyl alcohol and paint fluffy clouds randomly over cake top and sides. As you paint each cloud, sprinkle magic sparkles over while still damp (not wet).

5 Use the size guide to shape the baby's body from a size 16 ball of sugarpaste. Shape to a teardrop and curve slightly.

6 Shape the head from a size 14 ball of marzipan. Roll a ball and flatten slightly. Attach the body and head to the cake with glue. Dust the cheeks with pink powder colour.

7 Dip the tip of a cocktail stick into black paste colour and mark eyes. Mix a little isopropyl alcohol with brown paste colour and paint mouth.

8 Take a tiny ball of brown marzipan, place in the palm of your hand and start to roll a thin sausage. Get it as thin as possible and to measure 1.5cm long. Make a hole in the top of the head with a cocktail stick, push the strand of marzipan in making a little curl.

9 Roll out a small piece of modelling paste cut out the baby's shawl (pattern p35). Pleat together at the top and attach to baby's body folding the end under, sticking with glue. Cut two ends from pattern and attach to top of shawl.

10 Colour a size 11 ball of sugarpaste yellow. Keep enough for legs and feet then shape a long pointed beak from remaining paste. Attach beak across shawl joins.

11 Colour a small piece of modelling paste with gentian paste colour. Roll out and cut out a bow with the cutter.

12 Take a size 14 ball of sugarpaste and roll into a sausage shape. Make thinner at the neck and between tummy and tail area. Check the size against the cake, approximately 10cm long, then flatten slightly and attach next to beak.

13 Shape the first wing from a size 9 and attach. Shape the second from a size 11 and attach over first.

14 Dip the tip of a cocktail stick into black paste colour and mark eye. From remaining yellow sugarpaste shape two legs and feet then attach.

15 Soften a little sugarpaste with water. Place in a piping bag and trim end. Pipe over wings, tail and top of body. Using a damp paintbrush, spread icing over stork and then pull out icing with the damp paintbrush to give a feather effect.

16 Using a no.3 piping nozzle and a little royal icing coloured grey, pipe baby's name. Leave to dry. Mix silver powder with isopropyl alcohol and paint over name.

17 Dust shawl and underneath parts of stork with snowflake lustre.

Grace

20cm (8in) Rich fruit cake marzipanned and iced in Celebration Regalice and placed on a 30.5cm (12in) cake board, 450g (1lb) sugarpaste, a little royal icing, flower paste, Hint of Yellow Magic Sparkles ground finer (see p1) x 2 (JK), edible glue (p1), isopropyl alcohol.

Paste Colours: Egg Yellow (SF), Bulrush (SK).

Powder Colours: Dusky Pink (SF), Snowflake Lustre, Berberis, Silver, Sunflower (SK).

No.1 & 2 piping nozzles, straight frill cutter no.3 set 1 (FMM), Watermark Taffeta rolling pin (HP), frilling stick (Jem), cutting wheel (PME), size guide (see p1),(CC), assorted paintbrush and a flat dusting brush, non stick rolling pin and board.

1 Using the size guide, measure a size 12 ball of sugarpaste to keep white. Colour the rest of the sugarpaste pale yellow. Ice board. Roll out approximately 80g of this to 5mm thick. Cut out a circle with a diameter of 10cm. From this cut out a quarter section and then a piece straight across the bottom measuring 7cm (see diagram).

2 Smooth outside edge to a more rounded shape – but do not smooth cut edges of quarter. Emboss cradle with a no.2 piping nozzle. Using a flat dusting brush, brush some yellow powder colour on kitchen paper before brushing from the outside edge of the cradle in towards centre.

3 Brush centre of cake with a little glue and attach cradle. Mix isopropyl alcohol with yellow powder colour and paint dots. Roll a sausage of white sugarpaste from a size 8 ball. Point at one end and attach as a blanket along top edge of cradle.

4 Mix ¹/₂ yellow sugarpaste with ¹/₂ flower paste. Roll out a long strip and cut a piece measuring 15cm x 1cm. Frill with the frilling

stick then attach a piece down canopy and then along side of cradle with glue. When dry, dust cradle, frill and blanket with snowflake lustre.

5 Trace and cut out pattern for legs and rocker (p35). Colour a little flower paste brown then roll the watermark rolling pin over. Cut out using a cutting wheel and attach to cake.

6 Colour 20g of sugarpaste brown. For teddy's body shape a size 11 ball of sugarpaste and attach sitting on the rocker. His head is a size 10 flattened slightly. Feet are each a size 8, arms are each size 7, snout a size 7. Make ears from tiny balls of sugarpaste and hollow out before attaching. Mark down centre of snout with a knife then the mouth with the embossing tool. Colour a tiny piece of flower paste brown and attach for nose. Dip a cocktail stick in brown paste colour and mark eyes. Dust feet and sides of snout with pink dust.

7 Soften a little brown sugarpaste (see p1) and place in a piping bag. Cut off tip and avoiding snout, eyes and nappy area, work small areas at a time, pipe body, arms, edge of feet, face and edge of ears. Use a damp paintbrush to spread out icing and make fluffy for fur. Soften a little white sugarpaste and repeat in nappy area. When dry dust nappy with snowflake lustre. Shape nappy pin top from yellow sugarpaste and attach.
Colour a little royal icing grey and place in a bag with a no.1 nozzle. Pipe nappy pin. Pipe baby's name and date of birth.

8 Colour 100g of flower paste yellow to match sugarpaste. Knead it with 100g of sugarpaste. Roll out in a long thin strip and using the straight frill cutter on one edge, cut to a width of 4cm. Try to cut it in one piece to fit around cake. If you can't you can

disguise the join with softened sugarpaste. Attach around cake with glue.

9 Brush over board and side pieces thinly with glue. Place cake over a piece of greaseproof paper. Sprinkle over the magic sparkles. Remove excess and place back in pot.

10 Using grey royal icing and the no.1 piping nozzle, pipe a small plain shell around base of cake. Pipe hearts on to cake by piping two elongated bulbs and joining ends together.

11 When dry paint all grey royal icing silver with the silver powder colour mixed with isopropyl alcohol – name, date of birth, nappy pin, hearts and plain shell border.

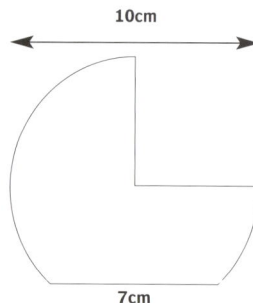

Harry

Fairy cakes baked in 'Rubber Ducky' baking cups (Wilton – PME), 2 packets of Rubber Ducky iced decorations (Wilton – PME), royal icing, 1 mini muffin cake – or a spare fairy cake, 110g (4oz) sugarpaste coloured egg yellow, small piece of flower paste, sieved apricot jam, 3 pots of Hint of Blue Magic Sparkles (JK), isopropyl alcohol, edible glue (p1).

Paste Colours: Gentian (SK), Paprika (SF).

Powder Colour: Black, Snowflake Lustre (SK).

Size Guide (see p1),(CC), Cupcakes 'n' more dessert stand (Wilton – PME), fine paintbrush, mouth embossing tool (Jem).

1 Colour the royal icing with gentian until it matches the hint of blue sparkles. Thin it down with water until it will spread over cakes and settle smoothly – similar to lightly whipped double cream. Spread icing over each fairy cake (leave spare one if using for duck's body

2 When surface of icing is almost dry, cover with magic sparkles. Push a rubber duck iced decoration into the top of each. Place the duck at an angle leaning slightly backwards. You may need to colour a small ball of sugarpaste gentian to place behind the leaning ducks as support.

3 Trim the mini muffin or spare cake to a round shape for duck's body. Spread thinly with jam then cover quite thickly with yellow sugarpaste. Shape paste out to a small pointed tail at the back.

4 Using the size guide measure three balls of sugarpaste each a size 7. Colour these pieces together with paprika to make orange. Divide back into three, shape two feet and attach to front slightly under body. Place body on to cake.

5 From two size 13 balls of yellow sugarpaste shape two wings. Flatten each slightly, point and curve upwards. Attach to body with a little glue. Emboss feathers on each wing with the mouth tool.

6 Roll a size 14 ball of sugarpaste for the head and attach to body. Make holes for eyes with a paintbrush handle. Brush holes with a little glue, then roll two small balls of flower paste for eyes and place in position.

7 Paint eyes with gentian paste colour mixed with a little water. Leave to dry then paint small black dots of powder colour mixed with isopropyl alcohol. Paint eyelashes.

8 Roll the remaining ball of orange sugarpaste for the beak. Flatten slightly. Press at one side to make flat to attach to face. Brush flattened side lightly with glue and attach to face. Mark two holes in beak with a cocktail stick.

9 Dust duck with snowflake lustre.

10 Leave all cakes to dry before assembling on cake stand.

Becky

20cm (8in) Round marzipanned and iced rich fruit cake, 30.5cm (12in) drum board, 350g (12oz) sugarpaste, flower paste or Mexican paste, 2 x white Magic Sparkles ground finer, (see page 1) (JK), royal icing, edible glue (p1).

Paste Colours: Rose, Gentian, Violet, Mint (SK)

Powder Colours: Snowflake Lustre (SK).

Triple curve 2cm ($1/2$ in) serrated crimper (PME), no.1 piping nozzle, Toys Tappits set (FMM), 2 flat dusting brushes, non stick rolling pin and board.

1 Place iced cake on board. Ice board and crimp around edge. Using a flat dusting brush, spread edible glue thinly over iced board. Place cake over greaseproof paper and cover board with sparkles. Remove cake from paper and place excess sparkles back in pot.

2 Roll a long thin sausage of sugarpaste and attach around base of the cake with glue. Crimp to match edge of board.

3 Colour four pieces of flower or Mexican paste with the four paste colours. Roll out the pink thinly and cut out approximately 14 dolls. Dry three over a curve to match the cake edge. Repeat with the other colours and shapes. Vary the position of the curves. Leave to dry.

4 Dust each toy with the snowflake dust.

5 Roll tiny balls of flower paste then attach two or three under each toy with glue. Leave to dry.

6 Pipe a little royal icing onto each ball of paste and start to attach the toys around the cake. Start at the bottom edge on the side and work your way round and over. Place toys between 1cm and 2.5cm apart.

7 Place royal icing in a bag with a no.1 nozzle and between the toys, pipe .....abc.....123.....abc.....123..... and so on.

8 If you wish to add a name, pipe it on the board, matching the colour to one of the toys.

David

20cm (8in) Round marzipanned rich fruit cake, 28cm (11in) drum board, 700g (1½ lb) sugarpaste coloured pale blue with Gentian paste colour (SK), 450g (1lb) sugarpaste coloured pale green with Mint paste colour (SK), 50g (2oz) marzipan coloured flesh with Paprika and Pink paste colours, Mexican paste, small piece of Teddy Bear Brown Regalice, 2 x Hint of Green Magic Sparkles, edible glue (p1), isopropyl alcohol, Trex, alcohol.

Powder Colours: Snowflake Lustre, Bulrush, Leaf Green, Marigold (SK), Dusky Pink (SF).

Baby mould (KD), small blossom cutter, Rabbit / Chick set (PC), size guide (see p1), (CC), sponge pad, non stick rolling pin and board, size 0 and size 4 paintbrushes.

1 Place cake on board, brush with alcohol leaving a 15cm circle in centre. Roll out blue sugarpaste and cover cake. Cut a 15cm circle of sugarpaste in centre and remove. Roll out green sugarpaste to same thickness as cut out circle. Cut out a 15cm circle. Brush marzipan in centre of cake with alcohol then place green circle over and smooth.

2 Brush board with glue. Roll out a long strip of green sugarpaste 4cm wide and use to ice board. Trim board edge then re-roll trimmings into a long thin sausage (approximately 4-6mm diameter) to fit around base of cake. Attach paste around base of cake with edible glue.

3 Roll out Mexican paste thinly and cut out approximately 80 small blossoms. Leave to dry then dust with snowflake lustre.

4 Grease a non stick rolling board and rabbit and grass cutter with Trex. Roll out white Mexican paste thinly – do not lift and turn. Place rabbit cutter on paste and press firmly around edge. Remove cutter and repeat four times more. Lay pieces on a sponge pad for 5-10 minutes.

5 Brush sausage of sugarpaste around base of cake with glue. Attach rabbits to the side away from the cake and resting on the board. Support with sponge or kitchen paper behind rabbits if leaning towards cake. Leave to dry.

6 Using the size guide, shape a size 13 ball of marzipan for the front of the baby and a size 13 for the back. Knead each piece well and roll into very smooth balls. Shape each piece into a carrot shape and starting with the wide end at the head, press into each mould. Trim any excess marzipan with a knife – the marzipan should not come over the top of the mould. Turn moulds over and pull back the sides to remove baby. Stick together with glue. Leave to dry.

7 Paint rabbits noses and inside ears pink with powder colour mixed with isopropyl alcohol. Mix brown powder with isopropyl alcohol to a very thin consistency and paint rabbits. Paint the grass as for rabbits but with leaf green powder colour. Dust blossoms in grass with snowflake lustre.

8 Paint green centre of cake and iced board thinly with glue. Cover with sparkle. Attach blossoms with glue around centre circle and randomly on board. When dry paint in a tiny yellow centre with marigold into blossoms on cake, board and sides of cake.

9 Shape two rabbits ears each from a size 6 ball of marzipan by rolling to make longer, then hollowing out with a paintbrush handle. Dust centre lightly with pink powder colour. Brush ends thinly with glue and attach to baby head, supporting if necessary.

10 Dust baby's cheeks lightly with pink dust. Add a small amount of isopropyl alcohol and use a fine paintbrush to paint lips. Paint eyebrows and eyes closed with bulrush. Paint hair around face.

11 Soften brown sugarpaste with water (p1). Place in a piping bag and cut off end to the size of a no.3 nozzle. Pipe a little under baby and attach to centre of cake. Pipe brown sugarpaste over baby's body (leave feet) and spread out with a damp paintbrush (no.4). Clean off paintbrush and then use it to pull out sugarpaste to resemble fur. Cover back of head, back of ears and around front of head in the same way.

12 Add a ball of white sugarpaste for a tail and cover with softened white sugarpaste repeating as previously.

Jessica

25cm x 20cm (10in x 8in) Oval rich fruit cake marzipanned and placed on a 36cm x 30.5cm (14in x 12in) oval cake board, 1.3kg (3lb) Celebration Regalice, 40g (1½ oz) marzipan, 100g (4oz) flower paste, a little royal icing, 2 x Hint of Pink Magic Sparkles ground finer (see p1) (JK), isopropyl alcohol, edible glue (p1).

Paste Colours: Pink, Paprika (SF).

Powder Colours: Dusky Pink (SF), Bulrush, White Satin, Silver (SK).

Multi ribbon cutter (FMM), small blossom cutter & small heart cutter (FMM), sleeping baby mould (KD), small raw silk rolling pin (HP), nursery set embossers (HP), stitch wheel & cutting wheel (PME), butterfly cutter (PC), no.1 piping nozzle, frilling stick (Jem), dusting brush, no.2 paintbrush, non stick rolling pin and board, size guide (see p1),(CC).

1 Place cake on board and cover cake then board with sugarpaste.

2 Emboss all over board with nursery set, butterfly, small blossom and heart.

3 Mix pink powder colour with isopropyl alcohol to a watery consistency. Using a no.2 paintbrush, paint embossing by touching the outlines with the brush. The colour should run quickly off the brush filling in details. Leave to dry then dust over with white satin.

4 Soften a little of the sugarpaste (see p1) and using a no.1 nozzle, pipe a small plain shell around base of cake.

5 Knead together 100g of flower paste and 100g of celebration sugarpaste. Keep 6g of this for baby's clothes. Colour the rest pale pink.

6 Set the ribbon wheel as wide as it will go using the wavy edge wheels and stitch wheels. Roll out the pink modelling paste and using the ribbon wheel, cut a strip long enough to fit around cake side. Pleat one end of the ribbon and attach to the top left of the cake. Take the ribbon around the cake going down to the board, trim to fit then pleat the end and take up the side to meet the beginning.

7 Roll out another long strip with the remaining pink paste and cut with the ribbon wheel, cut two pieces measuring 17cm (loops), 2 pieces 10cm (tails), and 1 piece 7cm long (knot). Take the 10cm pieces and cut ends diagonally. Pleat at opposite ends and attach with glue at side ribbon join on cake. Pleat each end of the 17cm pieces, fold and join ends with glue. Attach to ribbon then open loops and support with kitchen paper until dry. The centre piece should be pleated at both ends. Fold pleating over at one end, brush with a little glue and attach over top of bow. Brush opposite end with a little glue then fold under and attach over tops of tails. Leave to dry then brush thinly all over with glue and cover with magic sparkles.

8 Colour marzipan flesh with paprika and pink paste colours. Using the size guide roll two size 13 balls of marzipan. Roll two carrot shapes then starting with the wide end at the head, press into each mould. Trim any excess with a knife - the marzipan should not come over the top of the mould. Turn moulds over and pull back sides to remove baby. Stick together with glue and leave to dry.

9 Dust baby's cheeks with pink powder colour. Mix a little isopropyl alcohol with bulrush powder and using a fine paintbrush paint eyes closed and eyebrows. Paint hair (front only). Use a little pink colour to paint lips.

10 Trace and cut out pattern on page 34 for baby's clothes. Roll out the remaining 6g of modelling paste and use the silk rolling pin for the final roll. Lay pattern pieces over the paste and cut out using the cutting wheel. Frill the hem of the dress, sleeves and hat trim with the frilling stick. Run the stitch wheel along the top edge of frilling. Attach bonnet frill around inside edge of bonnet with a little glue. Brush head with glue then attach bonnet. Pinch together at back and then trim with scissors. Brush body with glue and attach dress, folding side edges under. Attach the sleeves and make another hem frill. Roll out some paste thinly and cut a thin bow for back of dress and attach.

11 Leave to dry then dust with white satin powder. Attach to cake with glue.

12 Colour a little royal icing grey and place in a piping bag with a no.1 nozzle. Pipe name and when dry paint with silver powder mixed with isopropyl alcohol.

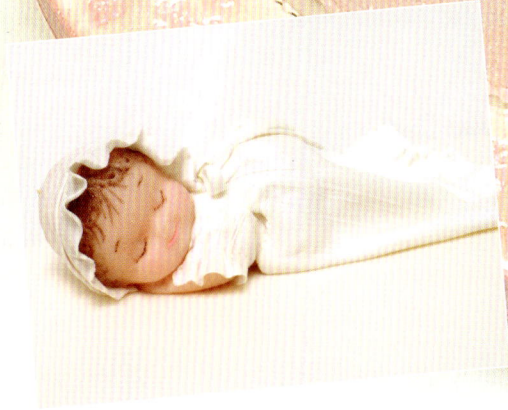

Stephanie

Duck sponge cake (see below), 1 muffin & 1 mini muffin, 30.5 cm (12in) cake board, 1.8kg (4lb) sugarpaste, flower paste, 3 x Hint of Lemon Magic Sparkles (JK), edible glue (p1), isopropyl alcohol, sieved apricot jam, spaghetti.

Paste Colour: **Sunflower, Berberis, Black (SK), Paprika (SF).**

Powder Colour: **Snowflake lustre (SK), Dusky Pink (SF), plus any four pastel shades.**

3-D Rubber Ducky Pan (Wilton - PME), small raw silk rolling pin (HP), 2cm (1/2 in) double curve serrated crimper, frilling stick (Jem), garrett frill cutter, ball tool, no.2 piping nozzle, Patchwork Squares Set (PC), Make a Cradle Set (PC), small scissors, paintbrush, large flat dusting brush, size guide (CC), dresden tool.

1 Check the quantity of sponge cake mixture you usually use with the tin size. Do this by filling each half of the duck tins with water and then pouring into your cake tins to see what size mix you will need. Follow the instructions given with the tins on how to use and bake.

2 Cover board with approximately 675g of white sugarpaste. Emboss square grid all over, then chosen patterns, small bear and stork in diagonal lines. Crimp edge of board. Dust patterned squares with pastel powder colours. Dust whole board with snowflake lustre.

3 Colour remaining sugarpaste yellow. Put 390g aside for wings. Brush apricot jam over cake. Roll out sugarpaste and place over cake. Shape in over head and down body. Any excess paste can be taken to back below tail point and trimmed away. Trim around base and smooth. Place on board. Hollow eyes with a ball tool.

4 Trim larger muffin to a more rounded shape for body. Colour the yellow sugarpaste trimmings a shade darker and shape a tail

from this to attach to the back of the muffin. Brush the muffin with apricot jam then cover the cake and tail with yellow sugarpaste. Place on board next to the large duck.

5 Trim the small muffin to a round shape. Cover with yellow sugarpaste. Attach head to body using edible glue and spaghetti. Indent for eyes with a ball tool. Roll out some flower paste and cut with a garrett frill cutter. Frill with the frilling tool. Cut out holes with a no.2 piping nozzle. Attach around small ducks face with glue. Roll out flower paste. Use the silk rolling pin for the final roll. Cut a strip measuring 16cm x 6.5cm. Check for size around ducks head (the back will be trimmed to fit). Trim where necessary then brush head with glue and cover with bonnet. Take excess paste to back, pinch together and then trim off with scissors. Crimp straight edge.

6 Colour a little sugarpaste black and roll small balls for eyes. Flatten slightly and attach. Mix a little snowflake with isopropyl alcohol and paint highlights to eyes. Paint black eyelashes.

7 Colour 110g of yellow sugarpaste orange by adding paprika. Roll a size 16 ball of sugarpaste using the size guide (see p 1). Shape to an oval and flatten slightly. Start to pinch and hollow out making the edges thinner. Pinch out more at the top and then to the left and right corners of beak. Brush cake with glue thinly over beak area and push orange paste over. Continue shaping and smoothing. Mark holes at top with a frilling stick. Emboss a line with a Dresden tool.

8 Shape the small beak from a size 12 ball of sugarpaste and attach with glue. Mark as before but use a cocktail stick for holes. Shape wedges of sugarpaste for large feet each from a size 13, the small feet each a size 8 and push under front of bodies. Roll out thin strips of flower paste and make a bow for small duck.

9 Shape the small duck's wing from a size 15 ball of paste and attach. The large ducks wings are each approximately 160g of sugarpaste. Shape, smooth and attach to body, placing her left wing over small duck's back.

10 Use a dusting or pastry brush to spread glue thinly over large duck. Avoid face and chest. Place over greaseproof paper and cover with Magic Sparkles. Brush excess sparkle off board onto paper with a dry brush. Tip sparkles on paper back in to pot.

Rachel

20cm (8in) Marzipanned rich fruit cake, 28cm (11in) cake board, 450g (1lb) Lilac Regalice, 450g (1lb) white sugarpaste, 50g (2ozs) modelling paste (p1), 60g (2$\frac{1}{2}$ oz) natural marzipan, a little royal icing, Hint of Lilac Magic Sparkles ground finer (see p1) (JK), edible glue (P1), isopropyl alcohol.

Paste Colour: Violet (SK).

Powder Colours: Snowflake Lustre, Silver, Chestnut, Bulrush, Berberis, Gentian, Violet, (SK), Dusky Rose (SF).

Multi Ribbon Wheel (FMM), stork and small teddy (Make a Cradle Set PC), Flower Embroidery Embossers (set 10 HP), small heart cutter (FMM), Teddy mould (FMM), plain bow crimper (PME), Teddy Bear's Picnic mould (DP), no1 piping nozzle, assorted dusting brushes, size 0 paintbrush.

1 Place cake on board. Knead 450g each of lilac and white sugarpaste together. Ice cake and board. Set the ribbon wheel with the wavy cutting wheels 2.25cm apart. Roll across top of cake marking lines. Before moving to the next, measure 2.25cm to keep the lines evenly spaced.

2 Emboss every other band with the flower embroidery embossers, then the band between with the stork, heart and teddy. Crimp around top edge of board with the bow crimper.

3 Colour some modelling paste with violet paste colour. Set ribbon wheel to 3cm wide, but this time, include the stitch wheels. After checking cake size, roll out a long strip of the modelling paste to fit around base of cake - approximately 1.02m long x 3.5cm wide. Cut out ribbon. Emboss along ribbon with mini flower embossers. Brush edible glue around base of cake sides, roll up ribbon then unroll and attach around cake.

4 Knead balls of marzipan then press into moulds. Trim away excess paste. Release from moulds and leave to dry. You will need four of the large teddy and two of each teddy from the teddy bear's picnic mould.

5 Dust all over cake with snowflake lustre. Brush board thinly with glue. Place over greaseproof paper then cover board with sparkles. Any excess can be poured back into the pot.

6 Roll out white modelling paste to approximately 5mm thick. Cut out shapes for mobile from pattern (p34 & 35). Roll and shape the hook from a thin sausage of modelling paste. Attach all to cake and cover with snowflake lustre.

7 Dust all bears paws, bottom of feet and inside ears with dusky pink. Dust bows in different colours. Dust all bears with chestnut powder. Mix isopropyl alcohol with bulrush and paint eyes, nose and mouth. Dust over all bears with snowflake lustre.

8 Place a little royal icing in a piping bag with a no.1 nozzle and pipe straight lines from mobile arms to the position for the teddy. Pipe a bulb of icing at the end then place teddy over. When all teddies are in position paint strings silver with isopropyl alcohol mixed with silver powder.

9 Pipe royal icing behind larger teddies and attach in each corner on board.

Anna

20cm (8in) Oval rich fruit cake, 700g (1½ lb) marzipan, 2.3kg (5lb 4oz) sugarpaste, 30.5cm (12in) cake board, flower paste, scintillo piping gel in silver (SK), white magic sparkles ground finer (see p1) (JK), edible glue (p1), isopropyl alcohol, a piece of spaghetti.

Paste Colours: Marigold, Gentian, Rose, Bulrush, Black (SK).

Powder Colours: Snowflake Lustre (SK), Dusky Pink (SF).

Square embosser from Patchwork Squares set (PC), mouth embosser (Jem), 2cm double curve serrated crimper (PME), Size Guide (see p1) (CC), no.2 piping nozzle, 4cm circle cutter, small sieve, paint and dusting brushes.

1 Cover board with sugarpaste. Trim and smooth around cut edges then emboss all over with the square embosser. Leave to dry then dust with snowflake lustre.

2 Turn cake upside down and trim 2cm from edge all round cake sloping sides out towards what will be the top of the cake. Turn cake over and cover with marzipan.

3 Colour 1kg (2½lb) of sugarpaste yellow. Roll approximately 160g of this into a long sausage to fit around top edge of cake. Secure with edible glue. Cover cake with yellow sugarpaste and place on board. Roll another sausage of yellow paste for bottom edge of bath. Attach and crimp both top and bottom edges.

4 Make bubbles from pieces of sugarpaste. Shape and attach one piece at a time with glue then emboss all over with a no.2 piping nozzle. When all are in place, dust over the whole bath and bubbles with snowflake lustre. Brush a little glue very thinly across bubbles and cover with magic sparkles.

5 Colour 200g of sugarpaste pink for the hippo. Make a pear shape from 90g and attach to board. Roll out a piece of white sugarpaste and cover lower half of body.

Using the size guide (see p1), shape each leg from a size 14 ball of sugarpaste and attach. Shape each arm from a size 12 and attach.

6 Shape top half of head from a size 14. Roll into and oval shape, flatten slightly, then slope lower half of this ready for the nose / mouth piece. Attach to the cake board leaving a 5mm gap from the top of the body. Shape an oval piece from a size 14 and attach between top of face and body.

7 Mark nose with the end of a paintbrush handle and mark a mouth with a circle cutter and eyes with a cocktail stick dipped in black paste colour. Make two small ears and hollow centres with a cocktail stick and attach.

8 Colour 100g of sugarpaste blue. Take a size 11 piece from this for the talc bottle, shape and attach to hippo. Roll a small ball of white sugarpaste and flatten a little for top. Mark around sides with a knife and attach to talc. Make holes in the top with a cocktail stick. Sprinkle a little icing sugar from a small sieve to give talc effect.

9 Using 80g of white sugarpaste, mould a pear shape for teddy's body and attach to board. Colour 140g of sugarpaste brown. Shape two legs each a size 13, two feet each a size 13 and attach. Arms are each a size 12. Shape and attach around to front of body. The head is a size 16. Mix a small piece of brown with an equal amount of white then roll into a ball, flatten and attach for snout. Mark mouth with the embossing tool and a line from mouth with a knife. Colour a piece of paste dark brown. Make holes for eyes. Roll small balls of paste for eyes and attach. Shape a triangle of paste for nose and attach. Dust soles of feet with pink powder colour.

10 Mix together 50g each of flower and sugarpaste. Roll out a small piece and cut a triangle to fit top of head and attach. Roll out remaining paste quite thinly and first cut out a square. Place over ted and pull round him to see where needs trimming to fit. When it will fit, brush teddy with a little glue, then wrap square tightly around him. From two balls of this paste, shape ears and attach. Leave to dry.

11 Soften some brown sugarpaste (see p1) and place in a piping bag. Pipe over teddy one area at a time ie leg, and spread with a damp paintbrush. Pull the icing up to give a fluffy effect.

12 Shape the rabbit's feet each from a size 14 ball of blue sugarpaste. Attach to board together against the bath. Shape a nappy from a size 15 ball of white sugarpaste. Attach over feet and push a piece of spaghetti through nappy and feet down to board. From a size 14 ball shape an oval for body and attach to nappy. Arms are each size 11. Shape and attach. The head is a size 15, ears are each size 9. Hollow ears with a ball tool. Attach head and ears. Mark mouth with the embossing tool pressed one way then the other. Roll a small ball of pink for a nose. Mark eyes as before. Attach a blue tail.

13 Soften white sugapaste and work over teddy's towel, hippo's nappy and rabbit's nappy as before for fur. Mix a little isopropyl alcohol with snowflake and paint a highlight to teddy's eyes and nose. Dust snowflake over towel and nappies when dry.

14 Mix some gentian paste colour into scintillo piping gel. Place in a piping bag and pipe into bath. Pipe a few splashes and drips over bath onto floor.

15 Shape a bar of soap and attach. The sponge is marked with a no.2 piping nozzle. Colour some sugarpaste yellow, a shade darker than the bath. Shape duck's bodies and wings from teardrop shaped pieces of sugarpaste. Add a ball for the head and mark eyes as before. Colour deeper again for the beaks. Attach and mark holes with a cocktail stick.

16 Shape a dummy from small pieces of sugarpaste, then talc as before and attach to board.

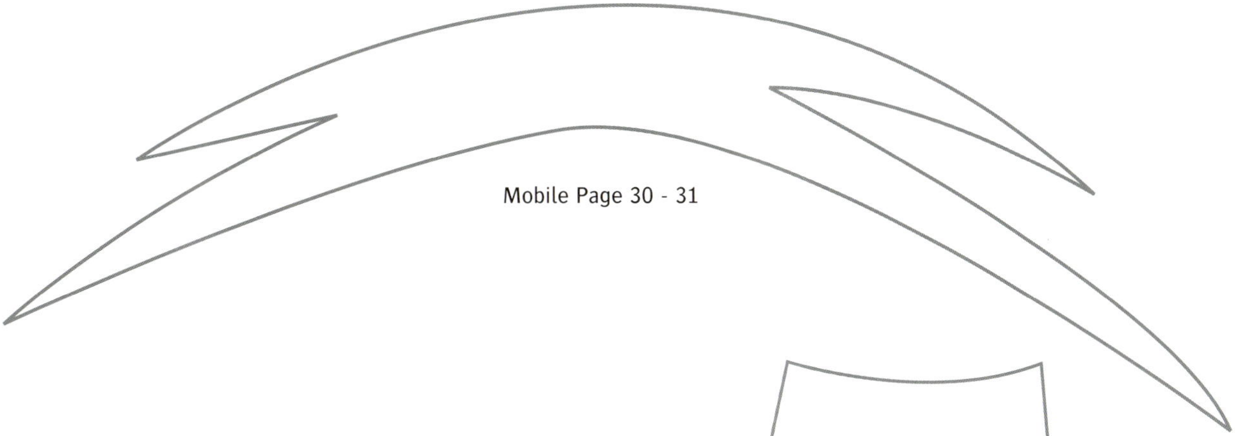
Mobile Page 30 - 31

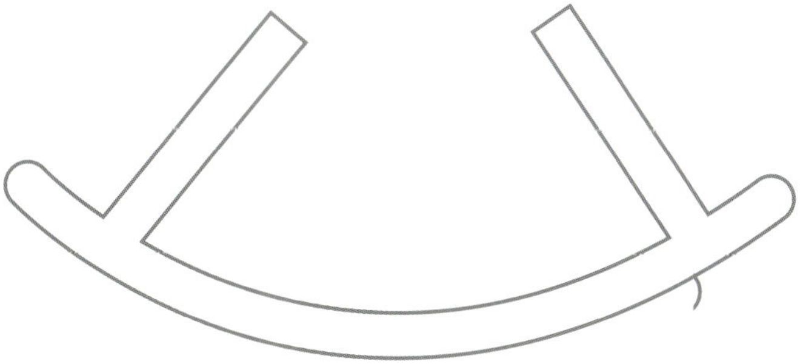

Grace page 18 - 19

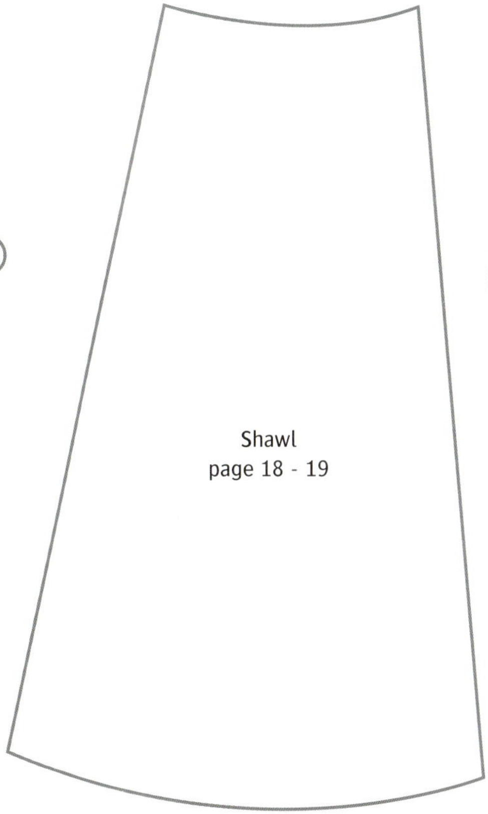
Shawl
page 18 - 19

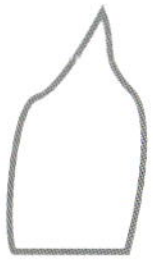

Cut 2

Patterns

Washing Line
page 2- 3

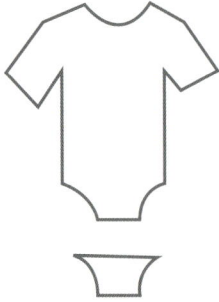

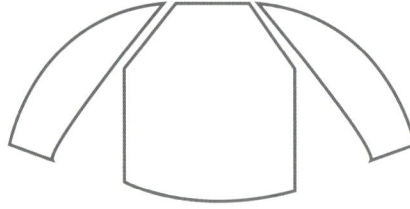

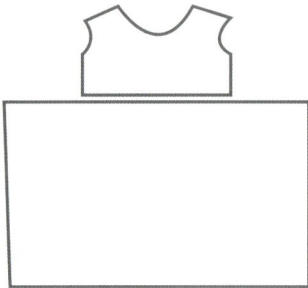

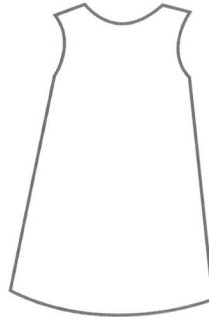